Alfred's Basic Piano Library

Prep Course

FOR THE YOUNG BEGINNER

Lesson Book • Level B

Willard A. Palmer • Morton Manus • Amanda Vick Lethco

Correlated materials to be used with *Prep Lesson Book, Level B:*

Cover art and interior illustrations by Christine Finn

A General MIDI disk [MIDI] (5717) and a Compact Disc (17160) are available, which include a full piano recording and background accompaniment.

Note to Parents and Teachers

Like Level A, the books of Level B continue at the proper pace for small children and take into consideration their normal attention span as well as their small hands.

The material introduced in these books has been carefully reviewed and tested, not only by the authors, but also by other experts in the field of music education who specialize in teaching young piano students.

The careful introduction of harmonic and melodic intervals under the span of the hands and the constant reinforcement of basic rhythmic patterns, lead to fluency in sight-reading beyond the results generated by most piano methods. The material is simple but tuneful, and is written especially to please students of this age group. The use of "overlapping concepts" provides more than adequate preparation for each new principle and insures problem-free progress without difficult gaps that might require the use of extra supplementary materials.

The PREP COURSE BOOKS are suitable for class lessons as well as private instruction. Upon completion of Level B, the student may continue into PREP COURSE, Level C, *or* ALFRED'S BASIC PIANO LIBRARY, Level 1B.

The authors and the publisher have endeavored to bring to the teacher and student the most attractive, enjoyable and practical approach possible. We sincerely believe that this course will open the vistas of the world of music to many young students who will continue to enjoy playing music for the rest of their lives.

THE PUBLISHERS

Outline of Basic Concepts in Prep Book B

Many pieces have DUET parts that may be played by the teacher, parent, or another student.

Contents

Circus Day!

C POSITION

1. Clap (or tap) & count.
2. Play & count.
3. Play & say note names.
4. Play & sing the words.

Follow these steps for each new piece.

Happily

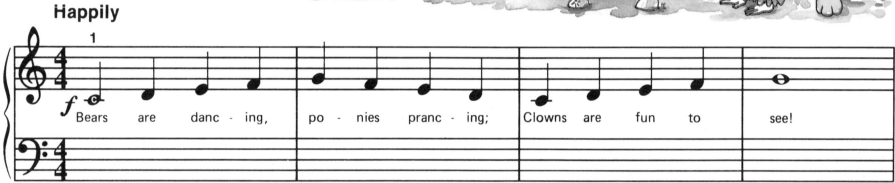

Bears are danc - ing, po - nies pranc - ing; Clowns are fun to see!

When the cir - cus comes to town, What fun for you and me!

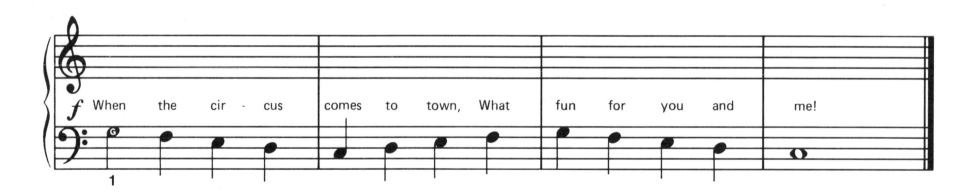

DUET PART

You are now ready to begin Prep THEORY, ACTIVITY & EAR TRAINING, CHRISTMAS JOY, and NOTESPELLER BOOKS, Level B.

Legato Playing

LEGATO means SMOOTHLY CONNECTED.
The notes are connected as smoothly as a rocking chair rocks.

SLUR

SLURS mean play LEGATO.

Slurs often divide
the music into PHRASES.

A PHRASE is a musical
thought or sentence.

Smoothly Rocking

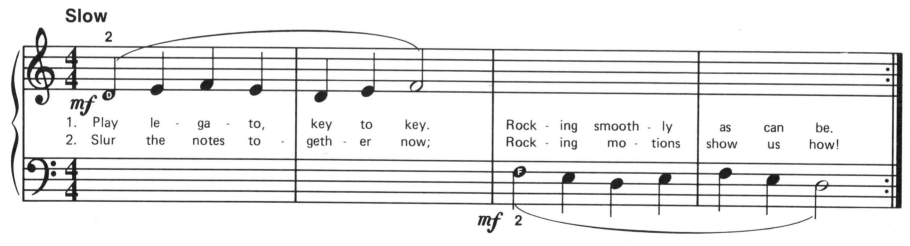

Slow

1. Play le - ga - to, | key to key. | Rock - ing smooth - ly | as can be.
2. Slur the notes to - | geth - er now; | Rock - ing mo - tions | show us how!

DUET PART (Student plays 1 octave higher.)

You are now ready to begin
Prep TECHNIC BOOK, Level B.

Row, Row, Row Your Boat

(RIGHT SIDE UP AND UPSIDE DOWN)

The 1st line is the familiar tune.

The 2nd line is the same, upside down!

Moderately slow

mf Row, row, row your boat, Don't fall in the stream!

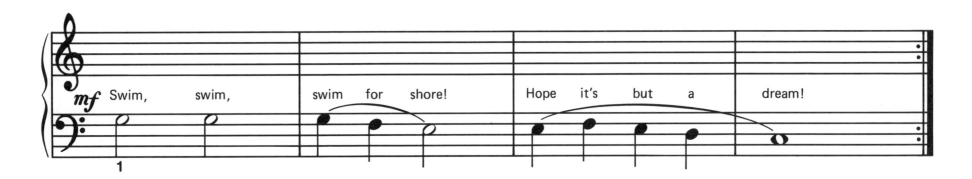

mf Swim, swim, swim for shore! Hope it's but a dream!

DUET PART (This is a ROUND, which begins 2 measures after the solo part begins, and ends 2 measures after the solo part ends.)

Measuring Distances in Music

Distances from one note to another are measured in INTERVALS, called 2nds, 3rds, etc.

 The distance from any white key to the next white key, up or down, is called a **2nd.**

2nds are written LINE-SPACE or SPACE-LINE.

Play, saying "UP a 2nd, DOWN a 2nd."   Play, saying "DOWN a 2nd, UP a 2nd."

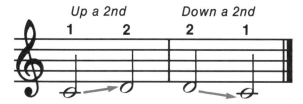   

Seconds

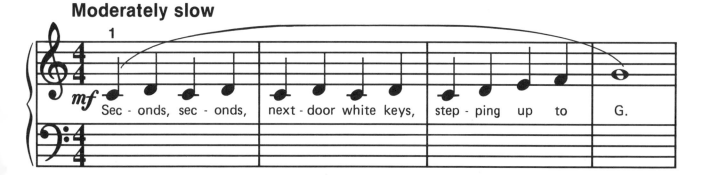

Moderately slow

Sec - onds, sec - onds, | next - door white keys, | step - ping up to | G.

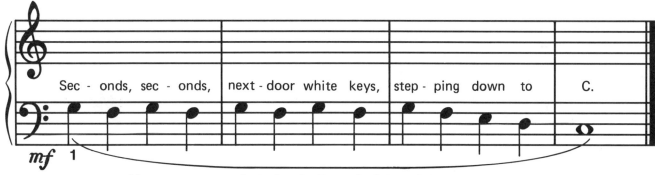

Sec - onds, sec - onds, | next - door white keys, | step - ping down to | C.

You are now ready to begin Prep SACRED SOLOS, Level B.

Gliding

Moderately slow

Glid - ing, glid - ing, high - er, high - er, Fly - ing in the sky!

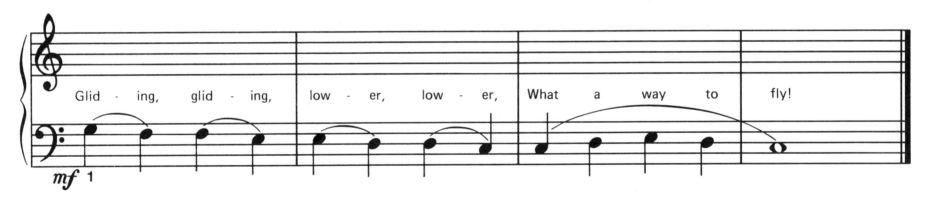

Glid - ing, glid - ing, low - er, low - er, What a way to fly!

DUET PART (Student plays 1 octave higher.)

You are now ready to begin Prep SOLO BOOK, Level B.

When notes on the SAME LINE or SPACE are joined by a curved line,
we call them TIED NOTES.

The key is HELD DOWN, not played again.

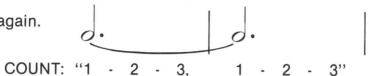

COUNT: "1 - 2 - 3,   1 - 2 - 3"

Balloons

Moderately slow

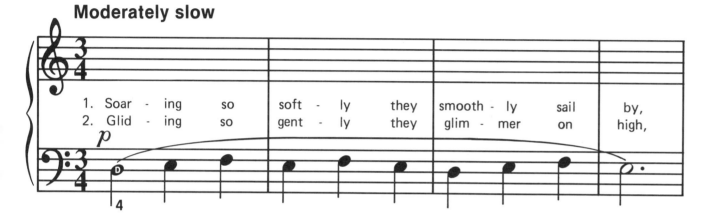

1. Soar - ing so soft - ly they smooth - ly sail by,
2. Glid - ing so gent - ly they glim - mer on high,

p

(TIED NOTES)

Float - ing like clouds as they fly.
Bright - 'ning the blue sum - mer sky.

p

DUET PART (Student plays 1 octave higher.)

When you skip a white key, the interval is a **3rd.**

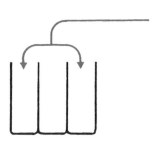

3rds are written LINE-LINE or SPACE-SPACE.

Play, saying "UP a 3rd, DOWN a 3rd."

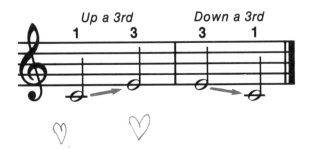

Up a 3rd 1 3 *Down a 3rd* 3 1

Play, saying "DOWN a 3rd, UP a 3rd."

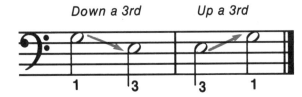

Down a 3rd *Up a 3rd*
1 3 3 1

Play a Third!

Moderately slow

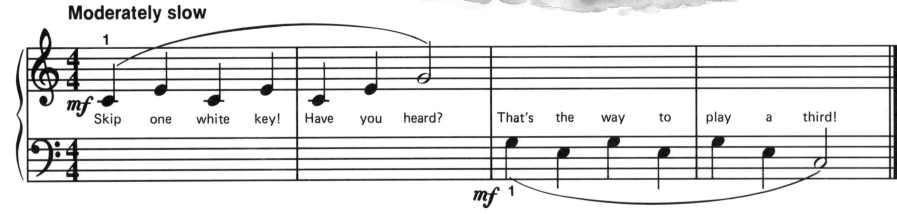

mf 1

Skip   one   white   key!   Have   you   heard?   That's   the   way   to   play   a   third!

mf 1

Come and Play!

Moderately fast

f Come and play! Come and play! We'll have lots of fun to-day!

p Come with me, and you'll see! *f* Come on out and play!

DUET PART (Student plays 1 octave higher.)

Hot Dog!

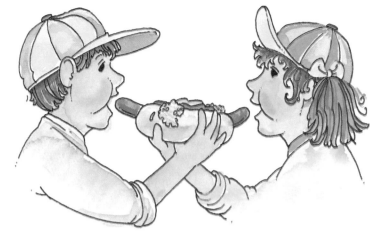

Happily

1. Hot   dog!   Hot   dog!   Or - der   me   a   hot   dog!
2. Hot   dog!   Hot   dog!   How   I   love   a   hot   hot   dog!

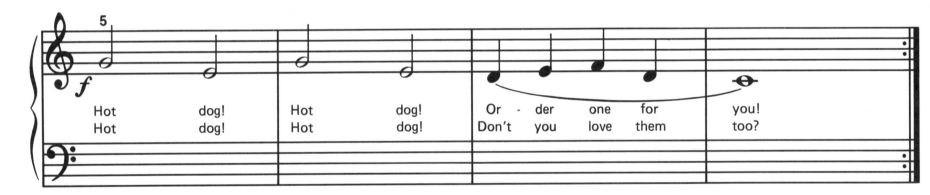

Hot   dog!   Hot   dog!   Or - der   one   for   you!
Hot   dog!   Hot   dog!   Don't   you   love   them   too?

DUET PART (Student plays 1 octave higher.)

What Can We Do?

Cheerfully

mf What can I do? What can you do? Just for fun, just for fun.

What can we do? What can we do? Just to have some fun!

DUET PART (Student plays 1 octave higher.)

More about Intervals

When notes are played separately they make a MELODY.

We call the intervals between melody notes MELODIC INTERVALS.

1. Play these MELODIC 2nds & 3rds. Listen to the sound of each interval.

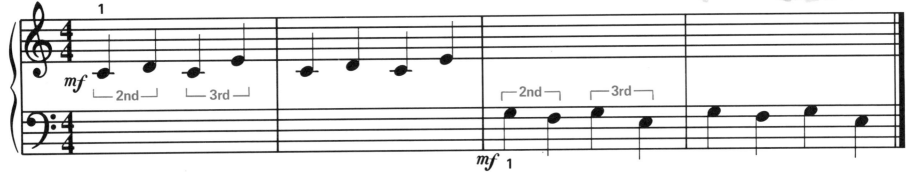

When notes are played together they make HARMONY.

We call the intervals between these notes HARMONIC INTERVALS.

2. Play these HARMONIC 2nds & 3rds. Listen to the sound of each interval.

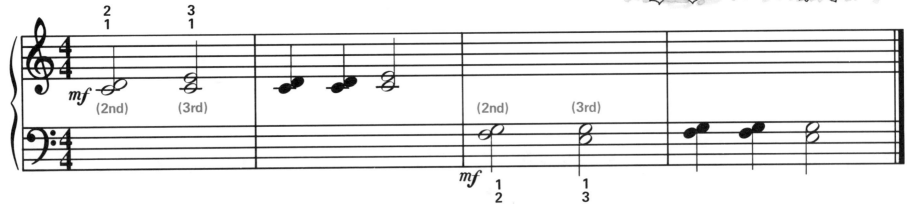

Pop Song

Brightly

1. Thirds with the left hand,
2. Thirds with the left hand,

Thirds with the right hand;
Thirds with the right hand;

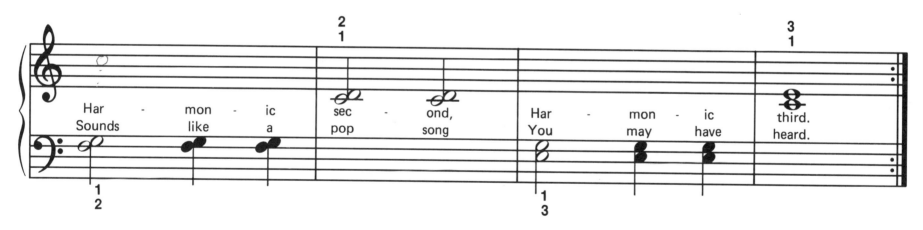

Har - mon - ic sec - ond, Har - mon - ic third.
Sounds like a pop song You may have heard.

DUET PART (Student plays 1 octave higher.)

RESTS are signs of SILENCE.

This is a **QUARTER REST.**

It means SILENCE FOR THE VALUE OF A QUARTER NOTE.

Taking Turns

4/day

Brightly

1. Right hand mel - o - dic! Left hand har - mon - ic!
2. Play with the right hand! Play with the left hand!

Right hand mel - o - dic! Left hand har - mon - ic!
Play with the right hand! Play with the left hand!

DUET PART (Student plays 1 octave higher.)

This is a **WHOLE REST.**

It means SILENCE FOR THE VALUE
OF A WHOLE NOTE
or any WHOLE MEASURE.

Quiet River

Moderately slow

Peace - ful riv - er, qui - et riv - er, gent - ly you flow.

Wind - ing slow - ly through the for - est, on - ward you go.

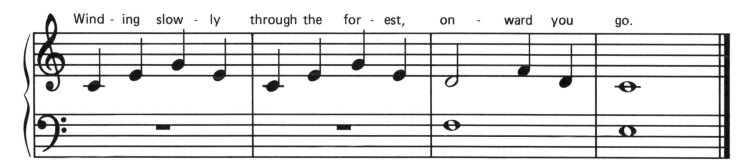

DUET PART

f — Loud
p. — Soft

Rockets

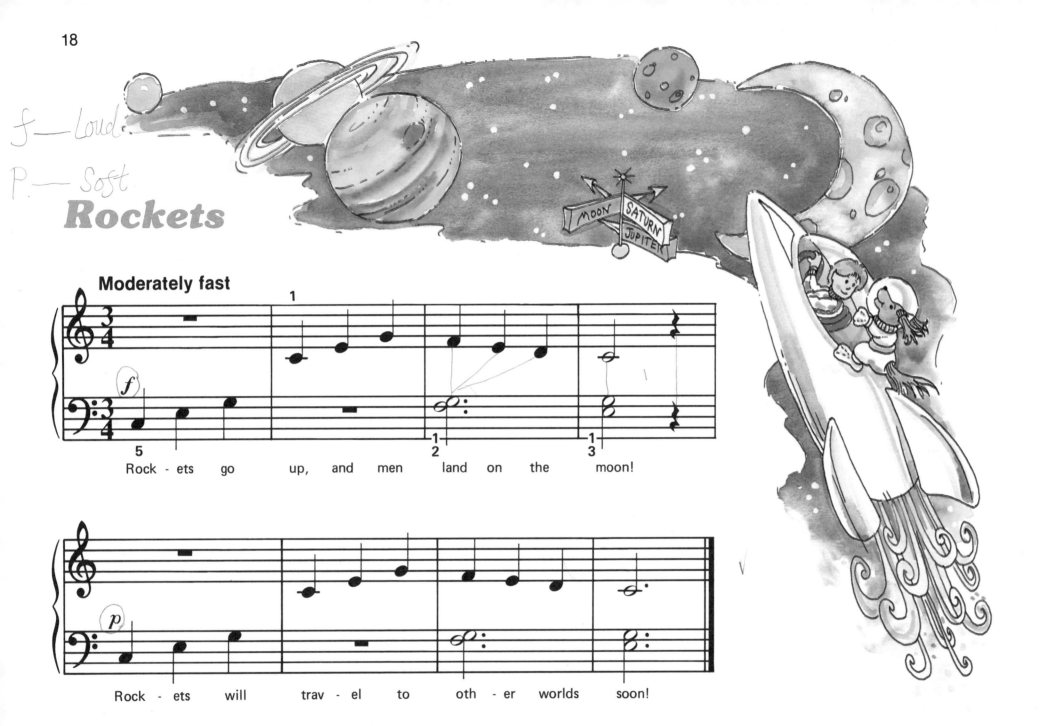

Moderately fast

Rock - ets go up, and men land on the moon!

Rock - ets will trav - el to oth - er worlds soon!

IMPORTANT! Play *ROCKETS* again, playing the 2nd line one octave (8 notes) higher.
The rests at the end of the 1st line give you time to move your hands
to the new position!

Sea Divers

Moderately slow

Down in the o - cean the sea div - ers go.

May - be they'll find man - y treas - ures be - low!

IMPORTANT! Play *SEA DIVERS* again, playing the 2nd line one octave lower!

When you skip 2 white keys, the interval is a **4th.**   4ths are written LINE-SPACE or SPACE-LINE.

Play, saying "UP a 4th, DOWN a 4th."

That's a Fourth

Moderately

Skip two white keys, that's a fourth. This is some-thing new!

I know how to play a fourth, Thirds and sec - onds too!

DUET PART (Student plays 1 octave higher.)

Let's Have Fun!

Moderately fast

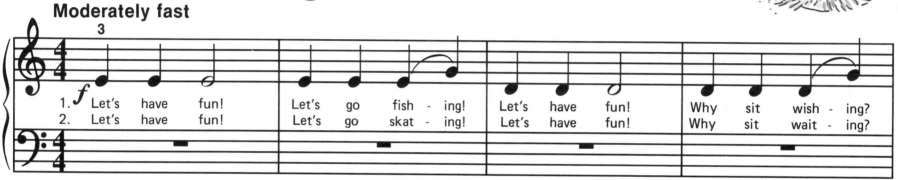

1. Let's have fun! Let's go fish - ing! Let's have fun! Why sit wish - ing?
2. Let's have fun! Let's go skat - ing! Let's have fun! Why sit wait - ing?

Let's have fun! Let's quit wish - ing! Let's go fish - ing all day long!
Let's have fun! Let's quit wait - ing! Let's go skat - ing all day long!

DUET PART (Student plays 1 octave higher.)

Love Somebody

Merrily

1. Love some - bod - y,   yes   I   do!   Love some - bod - y,   won't say who!
2. Love some - bod - y,   want to hear?   Let me whis - per in your ear.

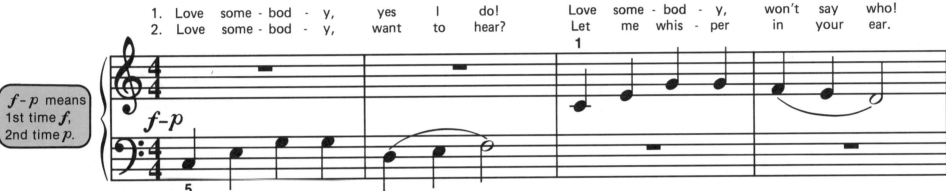

Love some - bod - y,   can you guess   Who's the one that I love best?
Love some - bod - y,   now you've guessed!   You're the one that I love best!

f **both times**

DUET PART

 This is a **HALF REST.**

It means REST FOR THE VALUE OF A HALF NOTE.

Showstopper!

Rhythmically, not too fast

1. I want to play a song that stops the show!
2. When I have played my song the world will know

I want to know be a hit, and that's be cause
That I know how a to get and some great ap plause!

DUET PART (Student plays 1 octave higher.)

(staccato)

Where Did You Get That Hat?

Happily

Where did you get that hat? Where, oh where? Where, oh where?

Where did you get that hat? I would like a hat like that!

DUET PART

Growing Up!

BEFORE PLAYING HANDS TOGETHER:

1. Play the left hand. Name each harmonic interval.
2. Play the right hand. Name each melodic interval.

Moderately slow

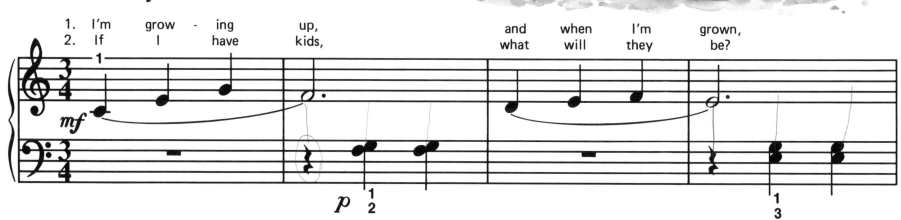

1. I'm grow - ing up,   and when I'm grown,
2. If I have kids,   what will they be?

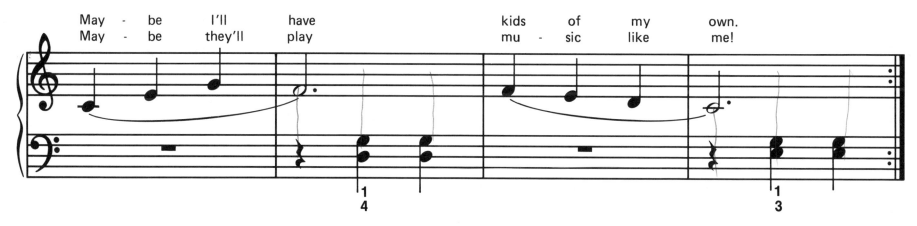

May - be I'll have   kids of my own.
May - be they'll play   mu - sic like me!

DUET PART (Student plays 1 octave higher.)

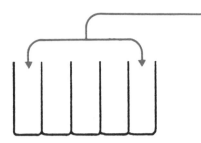

When you skip 3 white keys, the interval is a **5th.**

5ths are written LINE-LINE or SPACE-SPACE.

Play, saying "Up a 5th, DOWN a 5th."   Play, saying "DOWN a 5th, UP a 5th."

That's a Fifth!

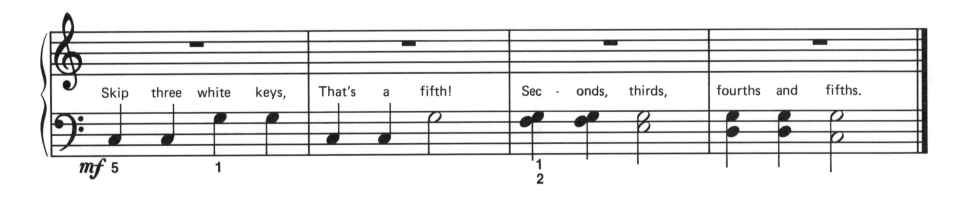

Moderately slow

Skip three white keys, | That's a fifth! | Sec - onds, thirds, | fourths and fifths.

Skip three white keys, | That's a fifth! | Sec - onds, thirds, | fourths and fifths.

What Will You Do?

Brightly

Both hands 8va (1 octave higher) 2nd time.

1. "What will you do when the meat's all gone?"
2. "What will you do when the lake all runs dry?"

"Sit in the cor - ner and gnaw on the bone!"
"Sit on the bank with a tear in my eye!"

DUET PART (Student plays 1 octave higher.)

Airplanes

Before playing hands together, play LH alone,
naming each harmonic interval.

Brightly

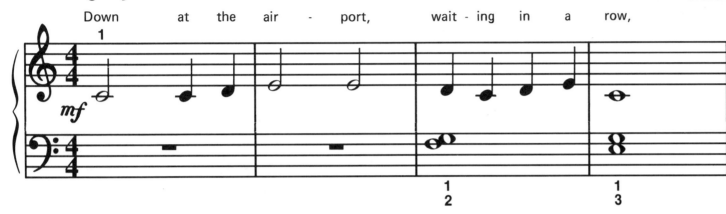

Down at the air - port, wait - ing in a row,

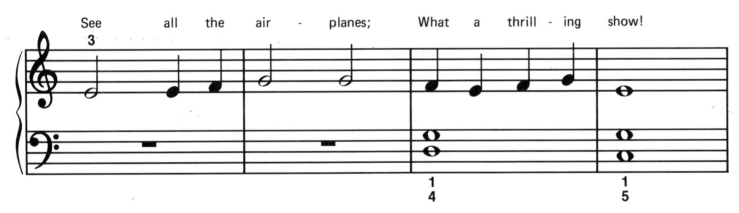

See all the air - planes; What a thrill - ing show!

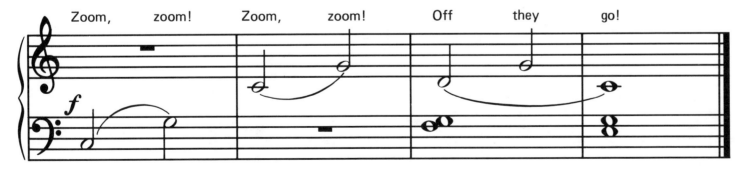

Zoom, zoom! Zoom, zoom! Off they go!

TEACHERS NOTE:
AIRPLANES may be played as a
ROUND for 2 to 4 pianos.
The 2nd piano begins after the
1st has played 4 measures.
The 3rd begins after the 2nd
has played 4 measures, etc.
Play 4 times.

Little Things

Moderately

Words by Julia A. Fletcher Carney

1. Lit - tle drops of wa - ter, lit - tle grains of sand,
2. Lit - tle deeds of kind - ness, lit - tle words of love,

Make the might - y o - cean, and the pleas - ant land.
Help to make Earth hap - py, like the Heav'n a - bove.

DUET PART

Both hands 8va

Playing in G Position

"Position G"

"G A B C D C B A," Gee, I like "po - si - tion G."

"G A B C D C B A," Gee, it's eas - y you'll a - gree!

"Moon-Walk"

G POSITION

Moderately slow

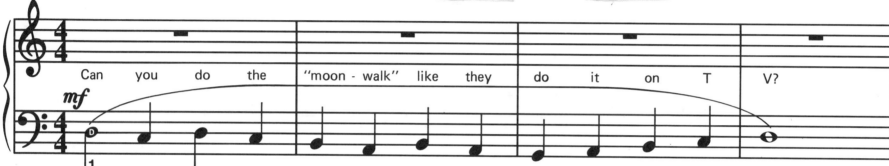

mf

Can you do the "moon - walk" like they do it on T V?

When they do the "moon - walk," it's a clev - er thing to see!

DUET PART (Student plays 1 octave higher.)

mf

Jingle Bells!

G POSITION

Merrily

f Jin - gle bells! Jin - gle bells! Jin - gle all the way!

Oh, what fun it is to ride in a one - horse o - pen sleigh!

Legato.

DUET PART (Student plays 2 octaves higher.)

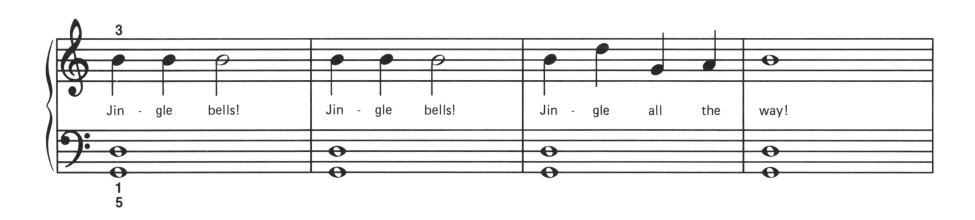

Jin - gle bells! Jin - gle bells! Jin - gle all the way!

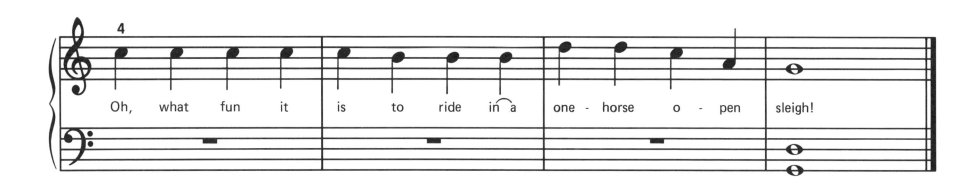

Oh, what fun it is to ride in a one - horse o - pen sleigh!

The SHARP SIGN
before a note means
play the next key to the RIGHT,
whether BLACK or WHITE.

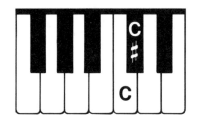

When a SHARP (♯) appears before a note,
it applies to that note for the rest of the measure.

Boogie Woogie Beat!

Moderately fast

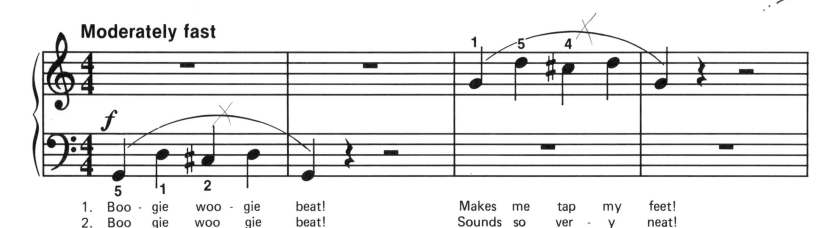

1. Boo - gie woo - gie beat!   Makes me tap my feet!
2. Boo - gie woo - gie beat!   Sounds so ver - y neat!

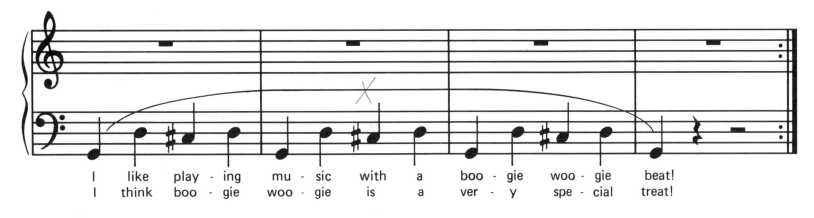

I like play - ing mu - sic with a boo - gie woo - gie beat!
I think boo - gie woo - gie is a ver - y spe - cial treat!

DUET PART

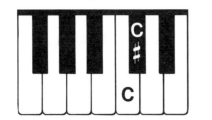 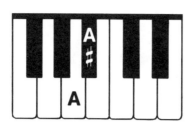

Make Time for Music!

Happily

1. Make time for mu - sic! Make time for play!
2. Make time for mu - sic! Make time for joy!

Take time to have a lit - tle fun to - day!
Ev 'ry new piece is like a brand new toy!

DUET PART

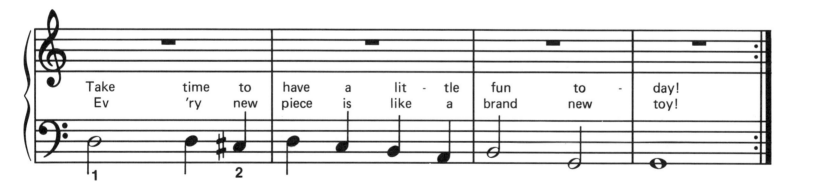

The FLAT SIGN before a note means play the next key to the LEFT, whether BLACK or WHITE.

When a FLAT (♭) appears before a note, it applies to that note for the rest of the measure.

Rockin' Tune

Moderately fast

1. *mf* If you're feel - in' blue, if you're feel - in' kind - a wea - ry,
2. Play this Rock - in' Tune, it will sure - ly make you cheer - y;

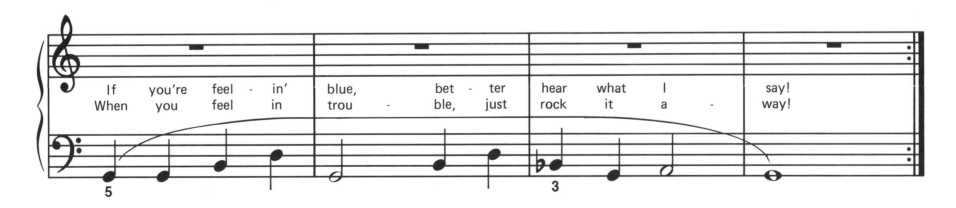

If you're feel - in' blue, bet - ter hear what I say!
When you feel in trou - ble, just rock it a - way!

Marching Song

Lively march time

Indian Song

Moderately, like tom-toms

1. I   go   where the In - dians go.
2. To   the   In - dians I'm a friend.

f-p

I   know   what the In - dians know!
We   are   broth - ers to the end!

f both times

Mumbo-Jumbo

Mysteriously

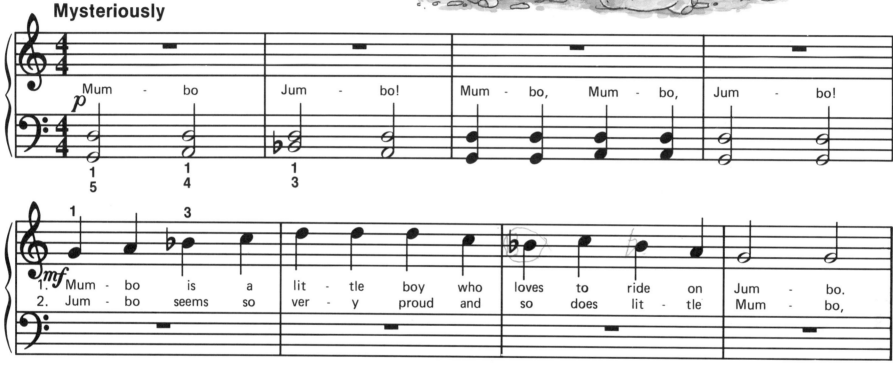

Mum - bo Jum - bo! Mum - bo, Mum - bo, Jum - bo!

p

1
5
1
4
1
3

mf
1. Mum - bo is a lit - tle boy who loves to ride on Jum - bo.
2. Jum - bo seems so ver - y proud and so does lit - tle Mum - bo,

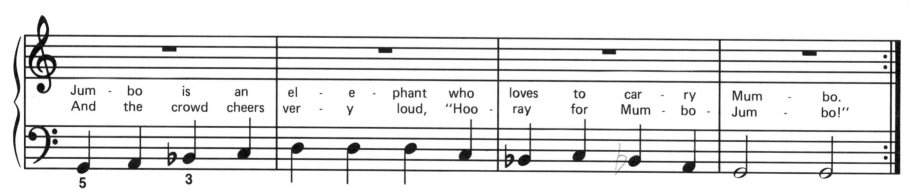

Jum - bo is an el - e - phant who loves to car - ry Mum - bo.
And the crowd cheers ver - y loud, "Hoo - ray for Mum - bo - Jum - bo!"

5
3

Suggestion: When playing at a recital or for friends, end *MUMBO-JUMBO* by repeating the first line twice, beginning *forte* and playing softer and softer as Mumbo rides Jumbo out of sight.

Staccato Playing

STACCATO means SEPARATED or DETACHED.

STACCATO is the opposite of LEGATO.
To play STACCATO, release the key the instant you play it.

STACCATO is indicated by a DOT over ♩ or under ♩ the note.

Raindrops

C POSITION REVIEW

Moderately

1. Pit - ter, pat - ter, see us scat - ter! Do the rain - drops real - ly mat - ter?
2. Scur - ry, scur - ry, bet - ter hur - ry! Drops of rain can make us wor - ry.

Hel - ter skel - ter, run for shel - ter, Just be - cause of drops of rain!
Drip and drop, the game must stop, and Just be - cause of drops of rain!

Cracker Jack!

Moderately fast

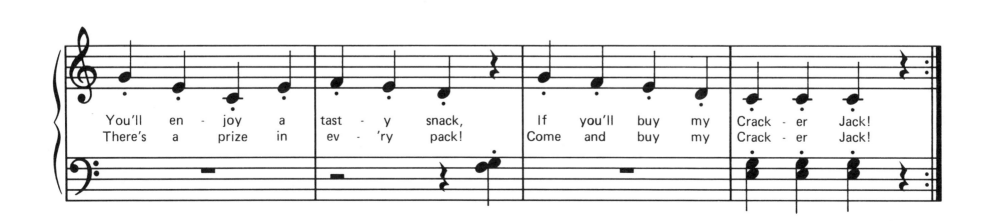

1. Come and buy my Crack - er Jack! By the pack! Crack - er Jack!
2. Come and buy my Crack - er Jack! Tast - y snack! Crack - er Jack!

You'll en - joy a tast - y snack, If you'll buy my Crack - er Jack!
There's a prize in ev - 'ry pack! Come and buy my Crack - er Jack!

NEW DYNAMIC SIGNS

CRESCENDO (gradually louder) **DIMINUENDO** gradually softer)

Hide and Seek

G POSITION REVIEW

Slow!

2nd time play both hands
1 octave (8 notes) lower.

1. When we're play - ing hide and seek, close your eyes, don't you peek!
2. When I hid be - hind the chair, you could not find me there!

You can hunt a day or week, You'll nev - er find me!
I can hide 'most an - y - where; You'll nev - er find me!

Anyone for Tic-Tac-Toe?

C POSITION REVIEW

Moderately fast

1. An - y - one for tic - tac - toe? Draw a sharp and here we go!
2. Just a game called "Tic - tac - toe." There's your X, and here's my O!

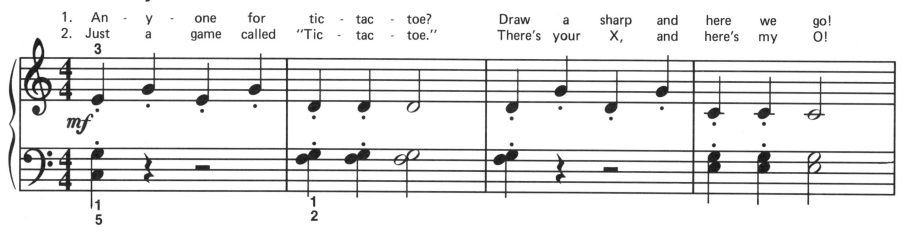

Lots of fun with X and O!
See my three O's in a row!

See who wins the game!
Now I've won the game!

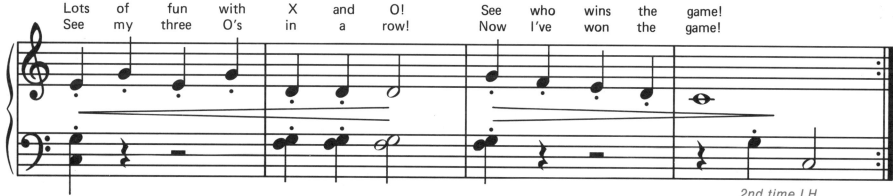

*2nd time LH
1 octave lower
on last 2 notes.*

DUET PART

Celebration

Happily

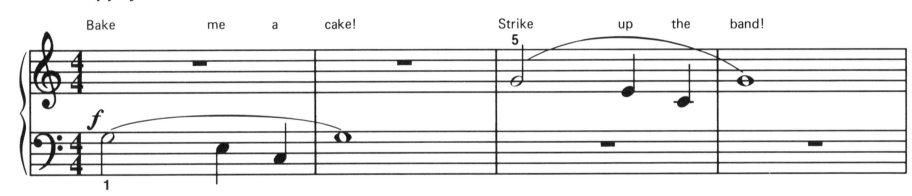

Bake me a cake! Strike up the band!

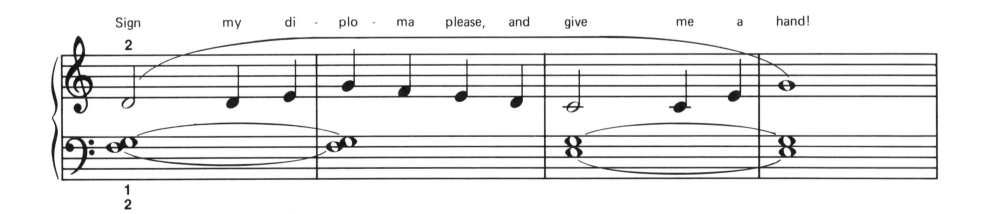

Sign my di - plo - ma please, and give me a hand!

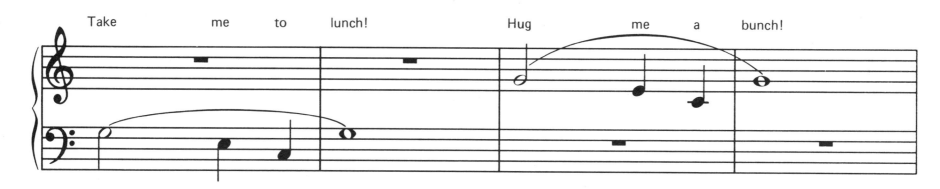

Take me to lunch! Hug me a bunch!

Slower

Now I will get a nice new book! Ta - dah!

Review

1. Match the rests with the notes by drawing a line from each rest to the note of the same value:

2. Name each of the following melodic intervals. Play each interval. Begin with RH 1.

3. Name each of the following harmonic intervals. Play each interval. Begin with LH $\frac{1}{2}$.

4. What is the meaning of each of the following dynamic signs?

p   *mf*   *f*   ⟨   ⟩

5. What is the meaning of f-p ?

6. ♯ This is a _____ sign. It means play the next key to the _____ .

7. ♭ This is a _____ sign. It means play the next key to the _____ .

8. Name each of the following notes. Play them all.

STACCATO   **LEGATO**

9. Which of the above means smoothly connected? _____

10. Which means separated or detached? _____

Certificate of Promotion

This Certifies that

Amy

has successfully completed
Prep Course Level B
and is hereby promoted to
Prep Course Level C

BASIC ALFRED'S PIANO LIBRARY

6-29   Jouese
_____   _____
Date   Teacher